SURPRISING MAMMALS OF THE ANCIENT ARCTIC

Nunavummi

The Nunavummi reading series is a Nunavut-developed levelled book series that supports literacy development while teaching readers about the people, traditions, and environment of the Canadian Arctic.

Published in Canada by Nunavummi, an imprint of Inhabit Education Books Inc. | www.inhabiteducationbooks.com

Inhabit Education Books Inc.
(Iqaluit) P.O. Box 2129, Iqaluit, Nunavut, X0A 1H0
(Toronto) 614 Mount Pleasant Road, Unit 1, Toronto, Ontario, M4S 2M8

Printed in Canada.

Library and Archives Canada Cataloguing in Publication

Title: Surprising mammals of the ancient Arctic.
Names: Hopkins, Dana, 1982- author. | Edzerza, Aaron, illustrator.
Series: Nunavummi reading series.
Description: Series statement: Nunavummi reading series | Written by Dana Hopkins, illustrated by Aaron Edzerza.
Identifiers: Canadiana 20220194440 | ISBN 9781774505489 (hardcover)
Subjects: LCSH: Mammals, Fossil—Arctic regions—Juvenile literature.
Classification: LCC QE881 .H67 2022 | DDC j569.0911/3—dc23

ISBN: 978-1-77450-548-9

INHABIT EDUCATION BOOKS

SURPRISING MAMMALS OF THE ANCIENT ARCTIC

WRITTEN BY

Dana Hopkins

ILLUSTRATED BY

Aaron Edzerza

What mammals live in the Arctic? You might think of polar bears walking across the frozen ocean. Maybe you think of caribou digging in the snow with their hooves, or seals swimming through icy water.

But did you know that mammals related to lions, hippos, and camels lived in the Arctic millions of years ago?

long ago

now

Today, the Arctic has short, cool summers. Lots of beautiful flowers and mosses grow close to the ground, but there are very few trees or other tall plants. Arctic winters are very long and cold. The land and water are covered in snow and ice.

But millions of years ago, the Arctic had warm summers and mild winters. Instead of rocky tundra, the land was covered in wet swamps and forests with huge trees. The **ancestors** of many familiar animals, such as bears, caribou, and seals, lived in the Arctic at that time. But there were also lots of other animals you might not expect!

ancestors: animals from the past that today's animals developed from.

HIGH ARCTIC CAMEL

Camels have thick fur and large, flat feet. They have one or two humps on their backs. Today, camels live in hot deserts in Africa and Asia.

Did you know that camels are originally from the Arctic? Scientists have found camel bones in what are now Nunavut and Yukon Territory, Canada. And those camels were big. They stood up to 3 metres tall. That's almost twice as tall as today's camels. They weighed over 800 kilograms. That's almost as heavy as two adult polar bears put together!

Giant camels lived in the Arctic about 3.5 million years ago. Back then, it was warmer in the Arctic. The land was covered in forests of very tall trees. Giant camels had teeth that helped them eat forest plants.

Scientists think that ancient camels had fatty humps on their backs, just like camels today. The fat probably helped them stay warm in the cold winters.

Also like camels today, giant camels had long legs and wide, flat feet. Their feet helped them walk in soft soil and snow long ago. Today, these feet help them walk in sandy deserts.

CORYPHODON

Hippopotamuses are large, heavy mammals that can open their mouths very wide. They have thick, grey skin with very little hair. They live near rivers, lakes, and swamps in Africa.

More than 50 million years ago, an animal that looked and behaved like the hippo lived in the Arctic. It was called the coryphodon. Coryphodons were about 1 metre tall and 2.5 metres long. They probably weighed at least 500 kilograms. That is more than an adult muskox!

Did You Know?

The coryphodon's brain weighed only 90 grams. It had one of the smallest brains for an animal its size ever discovered.

When coryphodons lived in the Arctic, the area was made up of swampy forests. There were massive trees growing out of warm water with lots of plants growing underwater.

Coryphodons were semi-aquatic. That means they lived partly on land and partly in the water.

Coryphodons had two pointy tusks that looked like fangs coming down from their upper jaws. In the summer, they used their pointy tusks to dig up plants underwater. In the winter, they ate dead leaves, twigs, and fungi like mushrooms.

MEGALONYX (GIANT GROUND SLOTH)

Sloths are small, furry mammals with long, strong arms. They live in trees in Central and South America and rarely come to the ground. They weigh less than 10 kilograms.

Eight million years ago, a massive ancestor of the sloth roamed the Arctic. The megalonyx, or giant ground sloth, had shaggy fur and long claws. It weighed about 500 kilograms!

Megalonyxes had very thick skin. They also had pieces of bone embedded in the skin on their shoulders, necks, and backs. These bony bits probably protected the sloths from the sharp teeth of predators.

sloth

megalonyx

Megalonyxes walked on all fours. They had a funny waddling way of walking. They could also stand up on their hind legs, using their strong tails to balance. This helped them reach high into trees and strip leaves and bark off branches to eat.

Megalonyxes had very soft teeth that never stopped growing. As they ate, the bark and leaves they chewed on would grind their soft teeth down to keep them short.

CHASMAPORTHETES (ANCIENT HYENA)

Hyenas are large animals that live in packs and hunt other animals to eat. They also eat dead, decaying animals. They live in Africa and Asia.

Over a million years ago, an ancestor of today's hyenas lived in what is now Yukon Territory, Canada. They are called chasmaporthetes and are also known as running hyenas. Chasmaporthetes lived in the Arctic during the last **ice age**, when there was snow and ice year-round. They probably had thick fur to help them survive the cold.

ice age: a time when thick ice sheets called glaciers cover huge areas of land.

hyena

chasmaporthetes

Chasmaporthetes were carnivores. They hunted animals like ancient caribou and maybe even young mammoths. They had very long legs that helped them chase their prey. They probably hunted on their own instead of in packs.

Chasmaporthetes had very sharp teeth. They also had powerful jaws that could crush bones. This allowed them to eat as much of an animal as possible, so they could get a lot of energy from one kill. Eating the entire animal probably helped them survive during the winter, when prey was harder to find.

STEPPE MAMMOTH (ANCIENT ELEPHANT)

Elephants are known for their large size, grey skin, long trunks, and big tusks. They live in Africa and Asia.

About two million years ago, large, hairy mammals that looked like giant elephants lived all over the Arctic. These were called steppe mammoths. Steppe mammoths were 4 metres or more in height and weighed 9000 or more kilograms. That's as much as a medium-sized airplane!

Did You Know?

Steppe mammoths are named after the kind of climate they lived in. A steppe is a habitat that is dry, flat, and covered in grasses.

Steppe mammoths had long trunks, like elephants today, with an extra flap of skin. Scientists think they might have curled their trunks up and tucked them under the flap to stay warm in the winter.

They also had huge tusks growing from the sides of their mouths. These tusks were 4 or 5 metres long and curved upward. Steppe mammoths probably used their tusks to dig up food in hard dirt. They might also have used them for fighting off predators.

ELASMOTHERIUM (ANCIENT RHINO)

Rhinoceroses have thick skin, large bodies, and horns that grow from their snouts. They live in Africa and Asia.

Millions of years ago, an ancient relative of the rhinoceros lived in the Arctic. They lived in an area of the Arctic that is now Siberia, Russia. Unlike rhinos today, the elasmotherium was covered in fur to help it live in colder climates. And instead of a horn on its snout, its horn grew from the top of its head. Some scientists think the horn was very large. Others think it was smaller.

Did You Know?

The elasmotherium's horn was made of layers of hard keratin, the same thing human hair is made of.

Did You Know?

The myth of unicorns might have come from ancient stories about elasmotheriums.

Elasmotheriums were 4.5 metres long and over 2 metres in height. They weighed about 4000 kilograms, more than twice as much as some species of modern rhinos.

These rhino ancestors ate plants. Like mammoths, they lived in grassy areas and along riverbanks. Their teeth helped them dig up grass and roots in moist river soil.

Elasmotheriums died out around 35 000 years ago. This means they were still alive at the same time as early humans.

CAVE LIONS

Lions are large wild cats that live in Africa. They are hunters that have golden fur, huge paws, and sharp claws.

Cave lions were fearsome hunters that lived in what are now Siberia, Alaska, and Yukon Territory. At over 2 metres long and 300 kilograms in weight, they were bigger than lions today. They had sharp teeth and claws and golden fur that was thicker and warmer than lions' fur today.

lion

cave lion

Cave lions lived in grasslands, forests, and mountains. They were ambush hunters. This means they would stay hidden until their prey got close and then attack it. They hunted animals like caribou and **cave bears**. In fact, cave lions got their name because they hunted in the dens of cave bears. When the cave bears were hibernating, the lions would attack.

cave bear: a species of bear that became extinct 24 000 years ago.

When we think of camels, rhinoceroses, and lions, we probably imagine them in warm climates, far away from snow and ice. It's hard to believe that long ago, ancestors of these animals roamed the Arctic! Scientists are still discovering the remains of ancient animals that once lived in the Arctic. What other kinds of animals do you think they will find?

Nunavummi

Nunavummi Reading Series

The Nunavummi reading series is a Nunavut-developed levelled book series that supports literacy development while teaching readers about the people, traditions, and environment of the Canadian Arctic.

Level 12

- 24–40 pages
- Sentences are complex and vary in length
- Lots of varied punctuation
- Dialogue is included in fiction texts and is necessary to understand the story
- Readers rely on the words to decode the text; images are present but only somewhat supportive

13

- 24–56 pages
- Sentences can be more complicated and are not always restricted to a structure that readers are familiar with
- Some unfamiliar themes and genres are introduced
- Readers rely on the words to decode the text; images are present but only somewhat supportive

Level 14

- 24–64 pages
- Chapter books introduced
- Readers may be exposed to new genres (science fiction, mysteries, biographies, etc.) and unfamiliar themes and settings
- Illustrations are somewhat supportive and may not be included on every spread of pages

Fountas & Pinnell Text Level: R

This book has been officially levelled using the F&P Text Level Gradient™ Leveling System.

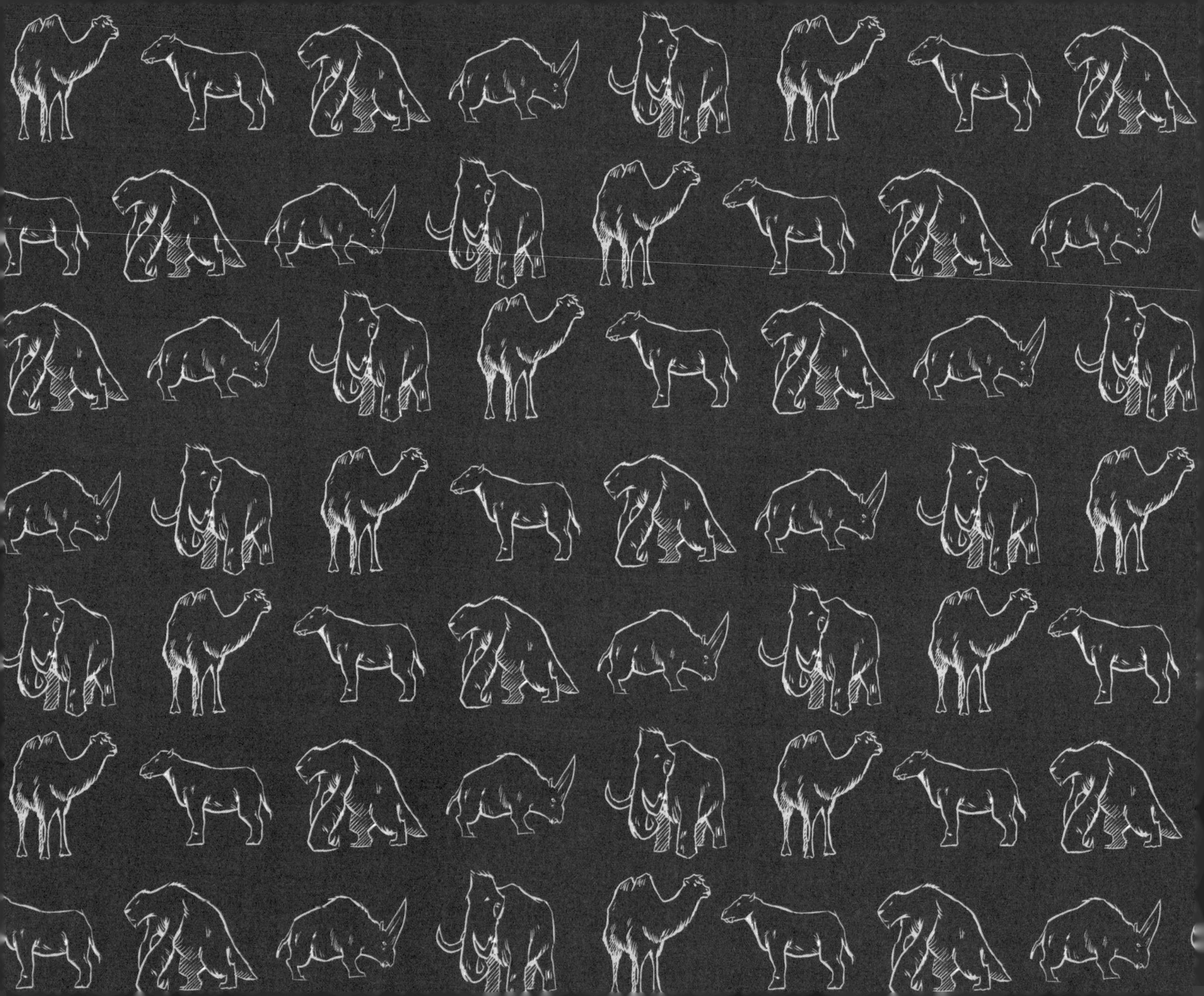

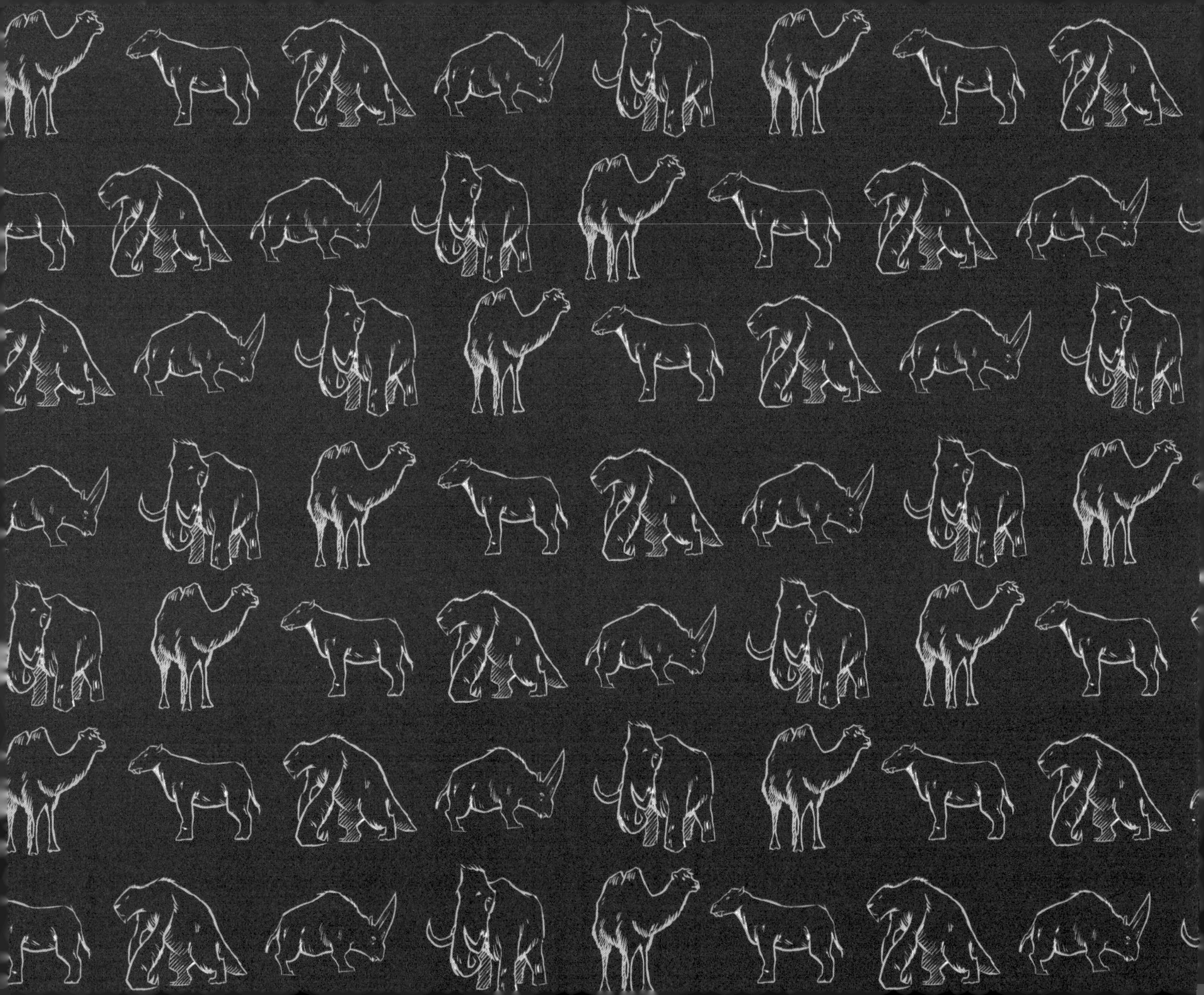